NFL TODAY

THE STORY OF THE ST. LOUIS RAMS

THE STORY OF THE ST. LOUIS RAMS

LORI DITTMER

CREATIVE EDUCATION

Cover: Rams defense, 1968 (top), Rams offense, 2008 (bottom)
Page 2: Wide receivers Isaac Bruce (left) and Torry Holt (right)
Pages 4–5: Rams defensive linemen, 1967
Pages 6–7: Running back Steven Jackson

....

Published by Creative Education
P.O. Box 227, Mankato, Minnesota 56002
Creative Education is an imprint of
The Creative Company
www.thecreativecompany.us

Design and production by Blue Design
Design Associate: Sarah Yakawonis
Printed in the United States of America

Photographs by AP Images (NBCU Photo Bank),
Corbis (Bettmann, Walter Bibikow/JAI), Getty
Images (Brian Bahr, Doug Benc, Andrew D.
Bernstein, Rob Brown/NFL, Michael Burr, Kevin C.
Cox, Nate Fine/NFL, Focus On Sport, Otto Greule
Jr, Kurt Hutton/Picture Post, Paul Jasienski, G.
Newman Lowrance, Lonnie Major/Allsport, Al
Messerschmidt/NFL, MPS/NFL, NFL, NFL Photos, Pro
Football Hall Of Fame/NFL, Roberto Schmidt/AFP, Vic
Stein/NFL, Kevin Terrell)

Library of Congress Cataloging-in-Publication Data

Dittmer, Lori.
The story of the St. Louis Rams / by Lori Dittmer.
p. cm. — (NFL today)
Includes index.
ISBN 978-1-58341-768-3
1. St. Louis Rams (Football team)—History—Juvenile
literature. I. Title. II. Series.

GV956.S85D58 2009
796.332'640977866—dc22   2008022699

First Edition
9 8 7 6 5 4 3 2 1

CONTENTS

X

X

ON THE SIDELINES

MEET THE RAMS

BORN IN
CLEVELAND

X--------

Situated on the bluffs that rise above the western banks of the Mississippi River, St. Louis, Missouri, stands just south of where the Mississippi and Missouri rivers meet. Founded in 1794, St. Louis boasts a history rich in adventure. In 1804, the famed Lewis and Clark expedition left the St. Louis area to explore the western United States. As settlers traveled through St. Louis using the Missouri River to reach the untamed frontier, the city earned the nickname "Gateway to the West." Today, tourists visit the city's famous Gateway Arch, a symbol of St. Louis history and the tallest man-made monument in the country.

Another popular St. Louis attraction, the Rams of the National Football League (NFL), has not always resided in Missouri. The franchise got its start in 1937 in Cleveland, Ohio, when the NFL expanded into a 10-team league. Homer Marshman, a Cleveland attorney and owner of the new franchise, named his team the Rams at the suggestion of the club's general manager, Buzz Wetzel. Wetzel had always admired the Fordham University Rams, and Marshman liked the sound of the name.

Johnny "Zero" Drake, a fullback known for his tough running and blocking, was the team's first draft choice. The Rams charged to their first regular-season win in September

X By the time the Rams finally made their way to St. Louis in 1995, "The Gateway City" was already home to big-league professional teams in the sports of baseball (Cardinals) and hockey (Blues).

This 1941 photo shows the early Rams' offensive backfield; of the group, running back Johnny Drake (second from right) and quarterback Parker Hall (far right) shone the brightest. **X**

1937 when they triumphed over the Philadelphia Eagles 21–3. It was the only win of their first season, but Drake continued to play well. During a game against the Detroit Lions in 1940, he scored a rushing touchdown, threw a touchdown pass, and rounded out his game by kicking an extra point. Another Rams standout of those early seasons was quarterback Parker Hall, who led the league in pass completions during his rookie season in 1939 and earned the NFL Most Valuable Player (MVP) award the same year. Despite these individual accomplishments, the Rams were unable to put together a winning season.

The Rams finally turned their record around in 1945. That year, the team drafted quarterback Bob "The Rifle" Waterfield, who immediately began leading Cleveland to

DAN REEVES

**TEAM OWNER
RAMS SEASONS: 1941–71**

Dan Reeves (pictured, left), the son of a New York City grocer, purchased the Cleveland Rams football team in 1941 for $100,000. When a reporter asked him why he made the purchase, Reeves said, "Doesn't every boy dream of owning a football team?" For the next 30 years, his innovative leadership influenced both the team and the NFL as a whole. He moved the Rams to Los Angeles in 1946, and to appease team owners concerned about the cost of traveling to the West Coast, Reeves offered $5,000 to each club that would come west to play. Reeves was the first owner to employ a full-time scouting staff, and he developed a scientific system for evaluating players that is still used. In addition, he arranged to have Rams football games broadcast in the early days of television. Reeves was one of three NFL owners appointed to finalize the details of the merger between the NFL and the rival American Football League in the late 1960s. He remained the team's owner until he died of cancer in 1971 at the age of 58.

HELMET HISTORY

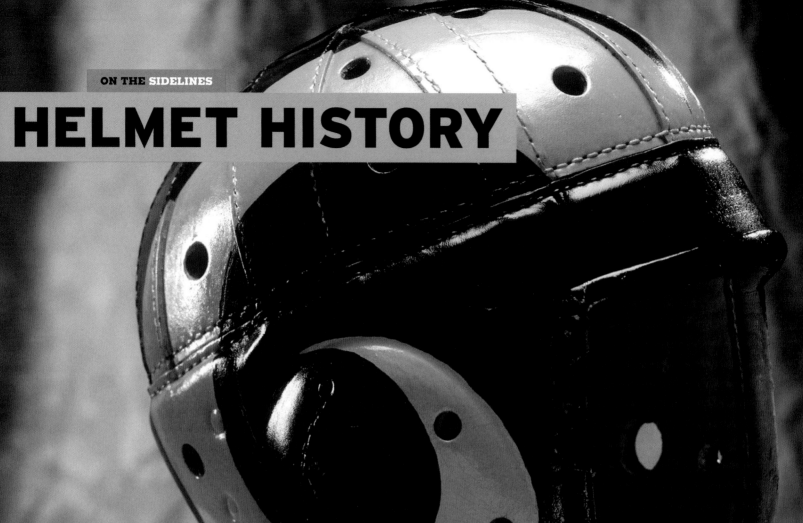

Today, NFL fans know which teams are on the field simply by looking at the players' helmets. But until 1947, helmets were not decorated. That year, a Los Angeles Rams halfback named Fred Gehrke proposed the idea of adding a design to his team's headgear. Gehrke had been an art major in college, and he sketched a picture of a curled ram's horn for the team's coach, Bob Snyder. Gehrke then painted the bright yellow design on a leather helmet to give Snyder a better idea of what the finished product would look like. Gehrke went on to decorate 70 leather helmets. The following season, everyone recognized the Rams by their headgear, as they were the first team to feature a helmet logo. Gehrke had the tedious task of maintaining the helmets, and he often took helmets home after games to touch up areas where the paint had chipped. The Rams began using plastic helmets in 1949, which made the paint less likely to chip and crack. Decals with adhesive backing became available in 1972. Today, all NFL teams except the Cleveland Browns display logos on their helmets.

victories. With a strong arm, tremendous accuracy, and a competitive spirit, Waterfield brought excitement to the game. After winning seven games in 1945, the Rams needed only one more win to top the NFL's Western Division, but Waterfield was ailing with a rib injury. Before the next game, against the Lions, a trainer told Rams head coach Adam Walsh that he couldn't use the quarterback. But Waterfield refused to be sidelined. "Tape me up and give

X The tough and confident Bob Waterfield rarely tried scrambling for yardage, instead relying on his strong throwing arm to pick apart defenses and move the Rams down the field.

me a shot!" he demanded. The Rams secured the division title with a 28–21 victory over Detroit. Waterfield led the way, connecting with end Jim Benton 10 times that afternoon.

As the Western Division champs, the Rams hosted the Washington Redskins in the NFL Championship Game. A blizzard blew into Cleveland, lowering the game-day temperature to a frigid two degrees. Unfazed, Waterfield tossed two touchdowns, one to Benton and the other to halfback Jim Gillette, to propel the Rams to a 15–14 win and the NFL championship.

In the frigid 1945 NFL Championship Game, players covered themselves in hay to try to stay warm on the sidelines; the next month, the Rams moved to sun-soaked Los Angeles. **X**

BOB WATERFIELD

**QUARTERBACK, DEFENSIVE BACK,
PUNTER, PLACEKICKER
RAMS SEASONS: 1945–52
HEIGHT: 6-FOOT-1
WEIGHT: 200 POUNDS**

As a rookie quarterback in 1945, the Rams' final season in Cleveland, Bob Waterfield (pictured, center) led the team to its first NFL championship, earning the league's MVP award in the process. The next year, the Rams moved to Los Angeles, where Waterfield led the team to three straight NFL title games. Known for his ability to throw the deep ball, Waterfield also demonstrated remarkable accuracy, earning him the nickname "The Rifle." Waterfield's sharp passing helped make the Rams one of the most feared offensive teams in the league. He remained calm no matter the score, and his determination often helped to rally his team to come from behind to win games. Although Waterfield was a quarterback, he contributed to the team in a variety of ways. For his first 4 seasons, he doubled as a defensive back, intercepting 20 passes. He also served as punter and placekicker, and his precise kicking netted 60 field goals and more than 300 points after touchdowns during 8 seasons.

A BOLD
MOVE WEST

X -----------------

Three weeks after the Rams won their first NFL title, owner Dan Reeves, who had purchased the Rams in 1941, announced that he was moving the team to Los Angeles. Reeves had lost money on the Rams in Cleveland, and he didn't want to compete with another Cleveland team, the Browns, who were part of a new league called the All-America Football Conference. At that point, no city west of the Mississippi River had been home to an NFL team. Other NFL owners expressed concern about the cost of traveling to the West Coast for games, but in the end, they approved the move.

X Halfback Kenny Washington scored just nine touchdowns in three seasons with the Rams, but his NFL career helped open doors of opportunity to other black football players.

In 1946, the Rams made history once again by signing halfback Kenny Washington and end Woody Strode, the first African American athletes to play in the NFL since 1932. During the late 1940s, the Rams had plenty of talent, but injuries kept them in the middle of the standings until 1949. By then, Los Angeles had acquired a sensational receiver named Tom Fears. "Fears was one of the greatest 'move' men in the history of the game," said Sid Gillman, who coached the Rams in the mid-1950s, of the receiver's array of moves on the field. "He didn't have much speed, but he could turn 'em on their heads."

The Rams also signed halfback Elroy "Crazylegs" Hirsch in 1949. Although the team already had two competent

receivers in Fears and end Bobby Shaw, head coach Clark
Shaughnessy changed Hirsch's position from back to end.
Assistant coach Hamp Pool developed the three-receiver
spread formation, which revolutionized the passing game.
Traditional defenses had a hard time keeping up with the
formation, and the Rams became one of the most potent and
exciting offensive teams in the league.

The Rams went 8–2–2 in 1949 and won the Western
Division. They then hosted the Philadelphia Eagles in the NFL
Championship Game. On game day, heavy rains flooded Los
Angeles, turning the playing field into a muddy mess. The
Eagles, who had dominated the season with an 11–1 record,
also dominated the game, winning 14–0.

In 1950, Joe Stydahar replaced Shaughnessy as head
coach, and he went to work polishing the Rams' running
game. Stydahar discovered that his three bruising
fullbacks—"Deacon" Dan Towler, Dick Hoerner, and Paul
"Tank" Younger—all of whom weighed around 225 pounds,
could run the ball well. He decided to use them together
in the backfield, and the trio, known as the "Bull Elephant
Backfield," gave the Rams a fearsome running game.

That same year, the Rams became the first NFL team
to televise all of their games, and they provided plenty of

X The Rams emerged as an offensive power in 1949, scoring an average of 35 points per home game at Los Angeles Memorial Coliseum.

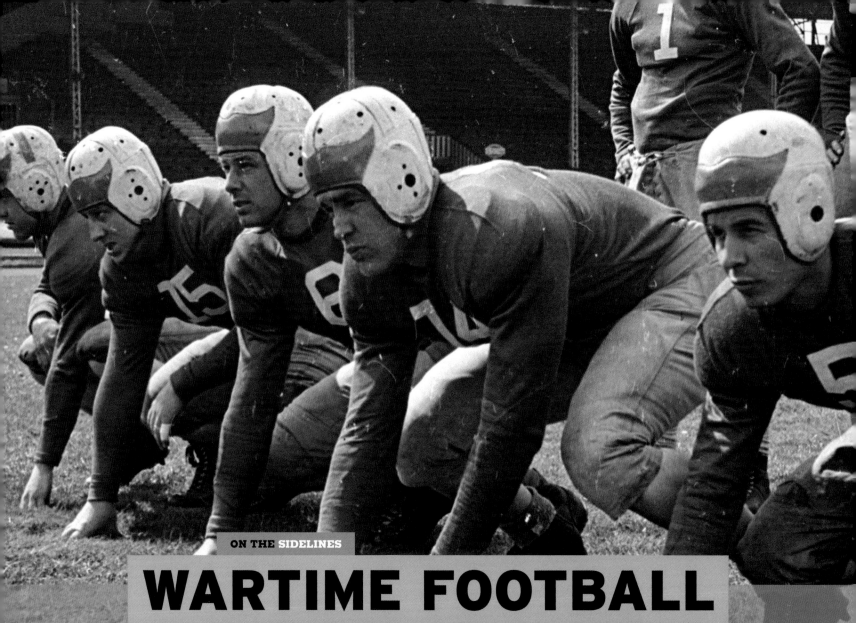

ON THE SIDELINES

WARTIME FOOTBALL

During World War II, nearly 1,000 NFL players served in some capacity in the United States military. The NFL considered canceling the 1942 season but decided to keep playing as best as the teams could. The Cleveland Rams felt the impact of the war most heavily in 1943. That year, some NFL teams merged to cope with the lack of players. But others, such as the Rams, suspended operations and did not participate in NFL games that season. Rams owners Dan Reeves and Fred Levy served in the U.S. Army Air Corps during the war. Reeves rose to the rank of captain before returning to football. In addition, Rams stars Norm Van Brocklin, Tom Fears, Bob Waterfield, Elroy Hirsch, and Parker Hall all served in the war. Twenty-three members of the NFL—including 21 active and former players, one team executive, and a former head coach—died in the war. Among them was Rams defensive back Frank Maher. The Rams resumed playing in 1944 with a still-depleted roster, finishing 4–6.

entertainment to viewers at home. The team was a scoring
machine. In one game against the Baltimore Colts, the Rams
scored 70 points, only 5 short of the 75 points the team had
scraped together during the entire 1937 season. The 1950
Rams scored 466 total points, setting a new league record
and clinching the National Conference. Unfortunately,
they lost the 1950 NFL Championship Game 30–28 to the
Cleveland Browns.

Quarterback Norm Van Brocklin, who had been drafted in
1949, then began splitting duties with the veteran Waterfield.
During the opening game of the 1951 season, Van Brocklin

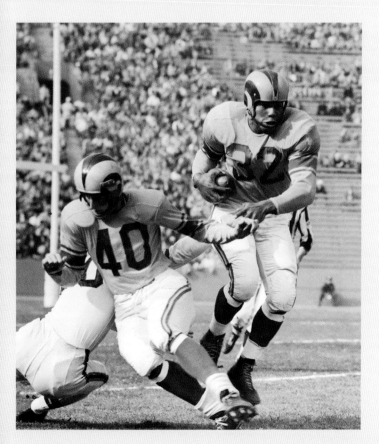

X Two stars of
the Rams' early '50s
glory years, speedy
Elroy Hirsch (left) and
brawny "Deacon" Dan
Towler (right) combined
to score 98 career
touchdowns for Los
Angeles.

filled in for an injured Waterfield and threw for an astounding 554 yards, setting an NFL single-game record. After winning their conference again, the Rams finally recaptured the NFL title. In the 1951 NFL Championship Game, Van Brocklin threw a 73-yard touchdown pass to Fears in the closing minutes to put the Rams over the Browns, 24–17.

The next year, a tough army veteran named Dick Lane joined the Rams. Lane arrived with limited football experience in high school, junior college, and the army, but after Coach Stydahar inserted him into the defensive lineup as a cornerback, the rookie set an NFL record with 14 interceptions on the season. Dubbed "Night Train" by his teammates and known for his teeth-rattling open-field tackles, Lane helped the team go 9–3 in 1952.

The Rams claimed one more conference title in 1955, then faced the Browns again in the NFL Championship Game. Van Brocklin, Hirsch, and Fears could not overcome the Browns, and the Rams fell 38–14. After that, the good times faded in Los Angeles. The Rams would enjoy only 1 winning season during the next 10 years.

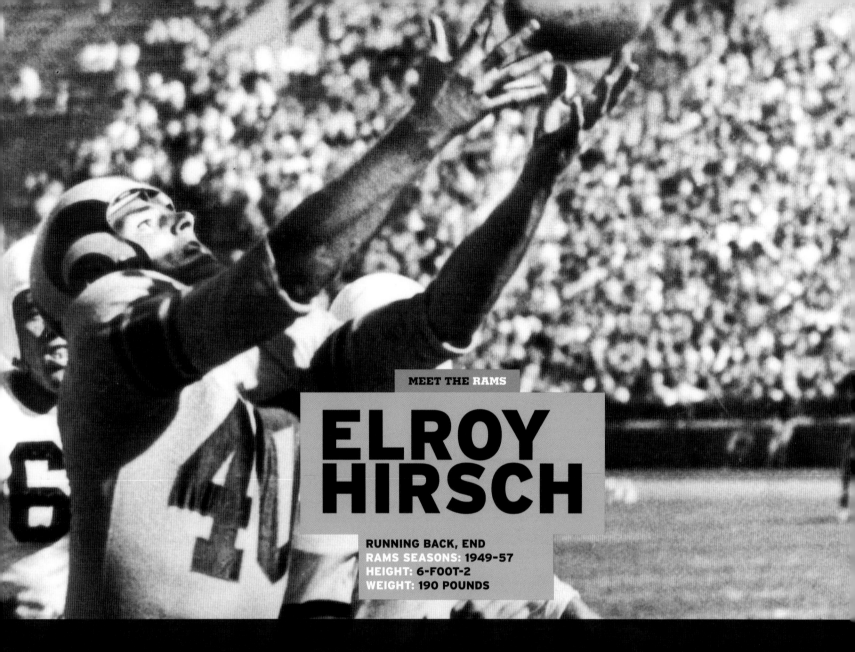

ELROY HIRSCH

RUNNING BACK, END
RAMS SEASONS: 1949-57
HEIGHT: 6-FOOT-2
WEIGHT: 190 POUNDS

Elroy Hirsch earned the nickname "Crazylegs" while playing high school football; when he ran, his legs appeared to whirl in several directions at once. Otto Hirsch, Elroy's father, once explained how the running style might have developed. "Elroy ran to school and back, skipping and crisscrossing his legs in the cement blocks of the sidewalks," Otto said. "He said it would make him shiftier." Hirsch joined the Rams in 1949 after three years of playing for the Chicago Rockets in the All-America Football Conference, where he suffered a variety of injuries, including a skull fracture. He sat on the bench for most of his first year with the Rams. Then coach Clark Shaughnessy shifted Hirsch to split end, and he became part of the team's famous three-end offense. Hirsch quickly gained attention with his ability to catch long-distance bombs from quarterbacks Bob Waterfield and Norm Van Brocklin. His style of catching the ball with his fingertips while running at full speed became known as the "Elroy Hirsch Special." After his playing days ended, Hirsch served as the Rams' general manager from 1960 to 1969.

[23]

DEFENSE
TAKES THE LEAD

In the early 1960s, the Rams acquired several new players who re-energized the franchise. Defensive end David "Deacon" Jones joined the team in 1961 and became one of the most intimidating pass rushers in NFL history. The following year, the Rams drafted quarterback Roman Gabriel and burly defensive tackle Merlin Olsen. In time, Gabriel became a successful passer and team leader, and with the help of running back Dick Bass, the Rams improved to 8–6 in 1966.

The Rams of the 1960s brought glamour and excitement to the defensive side of the ball. Jones and Olsen, together with tackle Rosey Grier and end Lamar Lundy, became known as the "Fearsome Foursome," a defensive line orchestrated by coach George Allen. The quartet made life miserable for opposing quarterbacks, and they quickly became fan favorites. During this time, Jones coined the term "sack" to describe tackling the passer behind the line of scrimmage. "We needed a shorter term," Jones said. "Like, you know, you sack a city—you devastate it."

A decade after reigning as the NFL's most explosive offensive team, the Rams—behind such players as Deacon Jones (number 75)—turned into a frightening defensive force. X

Los Angeles compiled a 32–7–3 record from 1967 through 1969. Although the Rams won the Western Conference's newly formed Coastal Division twice, they were unable to reach the Super Bowl (which was played for the first time in 1966), losing in the playoffs both times. As the 1970s began, the team remained a force. From 1973 to 1979, Los Angeles topped the National Football Conference (NFC) West Division (the league had been realigned again in 1970) each year. During that decade, the Rams' defense allowed fewer total yards and fewer points than any other team in the NFL.

The foundation of the team's strong defense in the '70s was end Jack Youngblood. A consistent league leader in sacks, Youngblood was tough and persistent. In 1979, he broke his leg in a playoff game against the Dallas Cowboys. Team trainers taped him up, and he returned to the game to sack Cowboys quarterback Roger Staubach in the fourth quarter. "Got me a sack on a cracked leg," he said. "There may not be too many guys who can say that!"

One week later, Youngblood wore a fitted leg brace that allowed him to play in the NFC Championship Game against the Tampa Bay Buccaneers. Scoring on three field goals, the Rams won 9–0 and moved on to face the Pittsburgh

POWER OF THE PEOPLE

Rarely do fans and players have much influence when it comes to the hiring and firing of professional football coaches. But in 1968, the people spoke up, and Rams owner Dan Reeves listened. Hired in 1966 as the Rams' head coach, George Allen built the team into a consistent winner. He assembled the famous "Fearsome Foursome" defensive line, and his first three seasons with the team produced a combined 29–10–3 record. However, Allen did not get along with Reeves, and fans were shocked when Allen was released on December 26, 1968. Roughly 7,500 people petitioned to save Allen's job, and nearly all of the team's players rallied behind him. In fact, six star players—including defensive end Deacon Jones and quarterback Roman Gabriel—threatened to retire if Allen was not reinstated. "He was a great motivator, and the players loved him," recalled Rams safety Richie Petitbon. Reeves relented and rehired Allen two weeks later. After two more winning seasons, Allen's contract expired, and Reeves did not renew it. Allen returned to the Rams as head coach briefly in 1978, but he was fired before the regular season even began.

Defensive end Jack Youngblood (left) never stopped hustling in pursuit of opposing quarterbacks; in 14 NFL seasons, he helped the Rams reach 5 NFC Championship Games. **X**

X A 6-foot-4 passer of Filipino descent, Roman Gabriel was the first Asian American to start as an NFL quarterback.

Steelers in Super Bowl XIV. Unfortunately, Youngblood's grit and determination were not enough to carry the Rams to victory. Although the Rams led 19–17 after three quarters, the Steelers pulled away to win 31–19.

FROM DICKERSON
TO EVERETT

The 1982 season was a forgettable one for the Rams. A players' strike cut seven games from the schedule, and the Rams finished last in the NFC with a 2–7 record. But the following year marked a dramatic turnaround for the Rams, who had acquired a new coach and a new star. The coach was former University of Southern California coach John Robinson, and the star was future Hall of Fame running back Eric Dickerson, who broke the NFL rookie rushing record in 1983 with 1,808 yards. "He made no noise when he ran," Robinson said in describing Dickerson's effortless-looking style. "If you were blind, he could run right by you, and I don't think you'd know he was there unless you felt the wind."

During the 1980s, the Rams advanced to the playoffs six times. In 1984, the club moved 50 miles southeast to Anaheim but kept its Los Angeles name. Three years later, the team's biggest star made a move of his own, as Dickerson was traded to the Indianapolis Colts. Still, quarterback Jim Everett kept the team on the winning track. In 1988, Everett led the NFL with 31 touchdown passes, many of them to receiver Henry Ellard.

Everett guided his team to an 11–5 record in 1989, and the Rams beat the Philadelphia Eagles and New York Giants to earn a trip to the NFC Championship Game against the San

X Eric Dickerson burst onto the NFL scene with a fury; in his first four seasons, he led the league in rushing three times and set an all-time record with an incredible 2,105 yards in 1984.

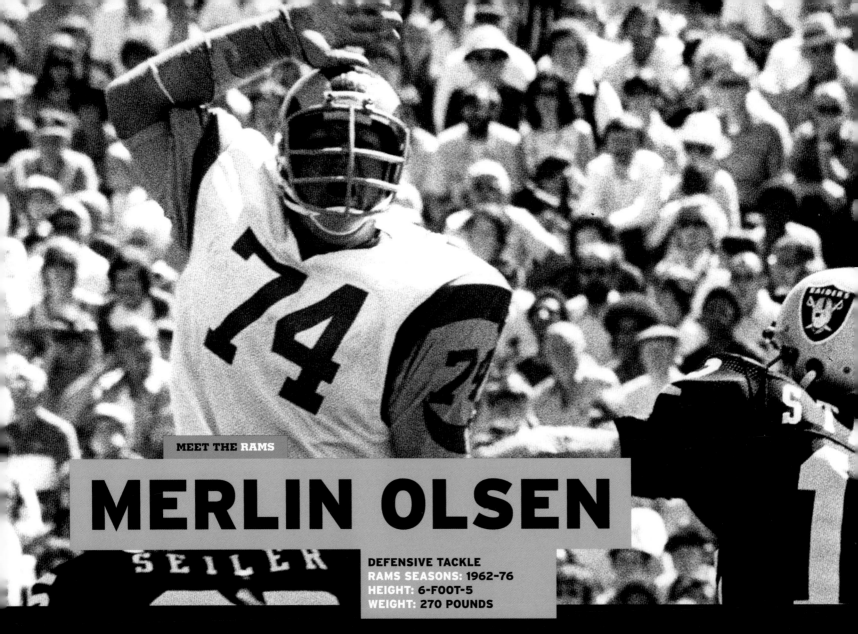

MERLIN OLSEN

DEFENSIVE TACKLE
RAMS SEASONS: 1962–76
HEIGHT: 6-FOOT-5
WEIGHT: 270 POUNDS

Rams players and fans alike looked up to Merlin Olsen. After all, at 6-foot-5 and 270 pounds, the defensive tackle from Utah commanded attention. In addition to his physical strength and size, Olsen was a smart leader and a dependable player. The Los Angeles Rams selected Olsen in the first round of the 1962 NFL Draft, and for the next 15 years, he proved to be one of the best defensive tackles of his time. The Rams' all-time leading tackler, Olsen racked up 915 stops. Early in his career, Olsen became the leader of a stout Rams defense that also included linemen Deacon Jones, Lamar Lundy, and Rosey Grier. Nicknamed the "Fearsome Foursome," the group wreaked havoc on opposing offenses throughout the 1960s, and the quartet's popularity sparked a new interest among fans in the defensive side of football. Olsen kept order along the line of scrimmage, and he felt a great responsibility to set a hard-working example for his teammates. "The winning team has a dedication," he once said. "It will have a core of veteran players who set the standards. They will not accept defeat."

Francisco 49ers. The game seemed to encapsulate the Rams'
decade of hope and disappointment, as Los Angeles fell one
win short of the Super Bowl, losing 30–3.

Then, in the early 1990s, the Rams began to flounder.
Although the team featured some exciting players, such as
fiery linebacker Kevin Greene and big running back Jerome
"The Bus" Bettis, the Rams posted a losing record every
season from 1990 to 1994. Fan attendance began to wane,
and the team struggled to find support for a new stadium. On

X An All-Pro as
just a rookie in 1993,
running back Jerome
Bettis combined raw
power with nimble
footwork like few
runners had before.

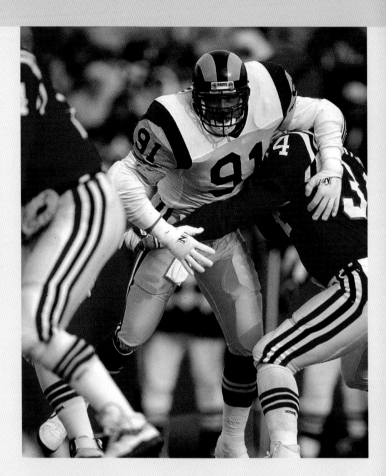

X Fast and fiery linebacker Kevin Greene sometimes lined up at defensive end, where he could better apply pressure to opposing passers.

Christmas Eve 1994, the team played its last game in Anaheim Stadium in front of just 30,000 fans.

Before the 1995 season, Rams owner Georgia Frontiere moved the Rams to St. Louis. On opening day, nearly 60,000 fans packed the city's Busch Stadium to welcome their new team, and the Rams rewarded their new fans by winning their first four games. That season was a special one for longtime Rams offensive tackle Jackie Slater, who reached a milestone as the first player in NFL history to play 20 seasons with one team. It was clear, though, that the team needed more talent, as the Rams went 7–9 in 1995 and 6–10 in 1996.

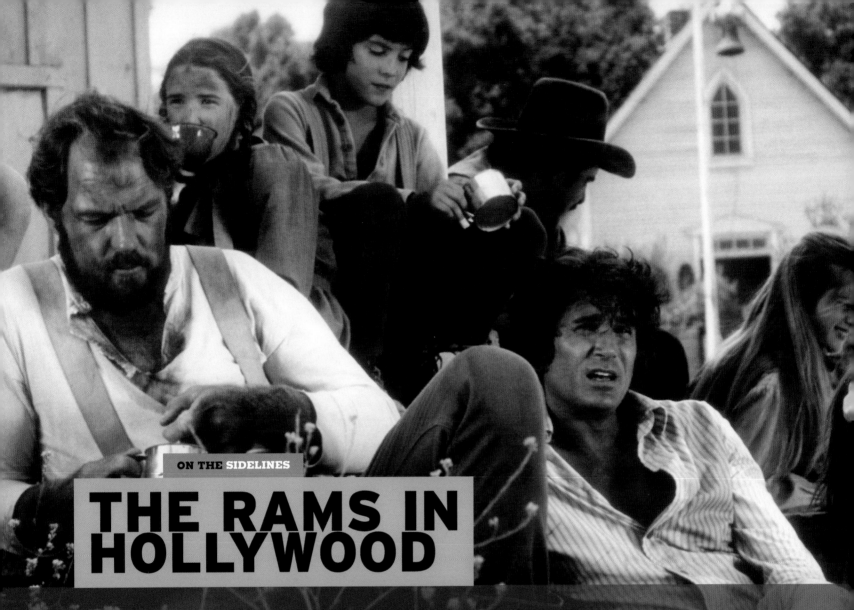

THE RAMS IN HOLLYWOOD

With their close proximity to Hollywood, the Los Angeles Rams drew a unique fan base of movie stars and producers. During the Rams' early years in California, quarterback Bob Waterfield was married to actress Jane Russell. "On team flights, you just waited to see if Jane was coming," noted Roman Gabriel, who had the quarterback job in the 1960s. Acting greats such as Henry Fonda and Kirk Douglas frequently attended Rams games. Elroy "Crazylegs" Hirsch, who captured fans' attention in the 1950s, also caught the eye of movie studios. He played himself in the movie *Crazylegs* and went on to appear in such films as *Unchained* and *Zero Hour!* Mike Henry, a Rams linebacker in the early 1960s, found Hollywood success playing the role of Tarzan. During the 1970s, Merlin Olsen, leader of the Rams' "Fearsome Foursome," played Jonathan Garvey (as pictured, left) in the classic television series *Little House on the Prairie*. Defensive end Fred Dryer, a key member of the Rams' defense in the 1970s, went on to star in the television detective series *Hunter* in the 1980s.

[35]

THE GREATEST SHOW ON TURF

In 1997, the Rams hired head coach Dick Vermeil, who came out of a 14-year retirement to take the position. Vermeil had been the Rams' first special-teams coach during the 1970s. The Rams added talented offensive tackle Orlando Pace in the 1997 NFL Draft, but they continued to struggle, going 5–11 in 1997 and a woeful 4–12 in 1998.

In early 1999, the Rams made a trade with the Indianapolis Colts for Pro Bowl running back Marshall Faulk, who was famous for his quickness. "He can go from a standing start to full speed faster than anybody I've ever seen," said former Indianapolis coach Ted Marchibroda. With Faulk lined up alongside veteran wide receiver Isaac Bruce, speedy rookie receiver Torry Holt, and quarterback Trent Green, the Rams were poised to make some noise in 1999.

During the 1999 preseason, when Green sustained a season-ending knee injury, the Rams were forced to put the offense in the hands of their backup quarterback, Kurt Warner. After playing college football at the University of Northern Iowa, Warner had not been drafted into the NFL. Instead, he played in the Arena Football League and in NFL Europe for four years before finding a backup spot with the Rams.

With Warner directing the offense and his fleet-footed teammates racing around the field, the fast-paced Rams

ERIC DICKERSON

RUNNING BACK
RAMS SEASONS: 1983-87
HEIGHT: 6-FOOT-3
WEIGHT: 220 POUNDS

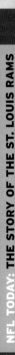

The Los Angeles Rams selected Eric Dickerson with the second overall pick of the 1983 NFL Draft. The team was committed to building a strong running game, and Dickerson did more than his part. In his first year, Dickerson set numerous NFL rookie rushing records, earning him a place in the Pro Bowl as well as the Rookie of the Year award. The following year, "Eric the Great" rushed for 2,105 yards—a league record that still stands. A powerful runner, Dickerson could tell when a defense was tiring, and his endurance often outlasted his opponents'. Although most running backs of the time kept their bodies low to the ground when they ran, Dickerson ran in a more upright position. He said he believed his stance helped him see better, and therefore, he could avoid taking big shots. "I don't give players a chance to hit me," he said. In 1987, the Rams, unwilling to negotiate when Dickerson asked for a new contract, traded him to the Indianapolis Colts, who paid a high price. To seal the deal, the Colts gave up two players and six high draft picks.

offense became known as "The Greatest Show on Turf."
Warner's success became one of the most unlikely stories
in NFL history, as he threw a whopping 41 touchdowns and
led St. Louis to a 13–3 record and the NFC championship. "I
told our team we could win with Kurt," said Coach Vermeil. "I
didn't expect that we'd win *because* of him."

The Rams met the Tennessee Titans in Super Bowl
XXXIV, a championship game that turned out to be one of
the most exciting ever. Warner threw for a Super Bowl-record
414 yards and connected with Bruce to break a 16–16 tie late
in the fourth quarter. On the final play of the game, Titans
quarterback Steve McNair fired the ball to receiver Kevin
Dyson at St. Louis's five-yard line. "When I saw the ball in the
air, I was terrified," said Vermeil. But his terror soon gave way
to joy, as Rams linebacker Mike Jones tackled Dyson about
one yard short of the goal line, securing victory for St. Louis.
The Rams had their first Super Bowl victory and third NFL
championship in franchise history. Two days later, Vermeil
announced his retirement.

The Rams remained a force in the following seasons,
making the playoffs in 2000, 2001, and 2003. Although both
Warner and Faulk battled injuries in 2000, the Rams finished
10–6 before losing in the first round of playoffs. The next

year, St. Louis came back strong, winning its first six games and finishing with a 14–2 record, the best in team history. The Rams then charged back to the Super Bowl, defeating the Green Bay Packers and Philadelphia Eagles along the way.

The Greatest Show on Turf was favored to win Super Bowl XXXVI over the New England Patriots. The Rams tied the game at 17–17 with 90 seconds left in the fourth quarter as Warner threw a touchdown pass to wide receiver Ricky Proehl. But the Patriots moved down the field with just enough time to kick a 48-yard field goal as the final seconds ticked away, giving New England the upset.

In 2002, Warner suffered a broken finger, and backup quarterback Jamie Martin was sidelined with a bruised knee. Thrust into a game against the undefeated Oakland Raiders, third-string quarterback Marc Bulger threw three touchdown passes and led the Rams to victory. Bulger's fine play sparked a quarterback controversy in St. Louis, and head coach Mike Martz ultimately named Bulger—who had become known for his deep, accurate passes—the team's permanent starter in 2003.

The Rams won the NFC West in 2003 with a 12–4 mark. In a playoff game against the Carolina Panthers, the Rams trailed 23–12 late in the fourth quarter before a Faulk touchdown run

STADIUM SHUFFLE

Throughout their nearly 75-year history, the Rams have made their home in three cities, but they have used many more stadiums. In the beginning, the Rams split their time between League Park and Municipal Stadium in Cleveland. They played four games at Cleveland's Shaw Stadium in 1938 and then continued going back and forth between League Park and Municipal Stadium, where they won the NFL championship in 1945. After moving to the West Coast, the Rams played at Los Angeles Memorial Coliseum, where they stayed for 33 years. It was there that the Rams made history in 1950 by scoring 70 points in one game—an NFL record that still stands—for a victory over the Baltimore Colts. The Coliseum hosted their second NFL championship win in 1951, when the Rams defeated the Cleveland Browns 24–17. In 1980, the Rams began playing in Anaheim Stadium, where they stayed until their 1995 move to St. Louis. After a brief stint in Busch Stadium, the Rams settled into the indoor Edward Jones Dome (pictured), where they completed a perfect 10–0 record at home in 1999.

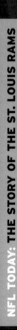
ON THE **SIDELINES**

THE FIRST OVERTIME

A preseason game between the Los Angeles Rams and the New York Giants on August 28, 1955, reshaped the rules of professional football. Prior to the game, the league had given permission to try the concept of overtime play, if needed. After the Giants scored twice in the first quarter, Rams fullback Paul "Tank" Younger found the end zone with a five-yard run, making the score 10–7 at halftime. With a field goal and another score, the Rams took a 17–10 lead, but the Giants tied the game in the middle of the fourth quarter. Until that game, professional football had not ventured into overtime, instead ending games in a tie. The Rams won the coin toss and so received the overtime kickoff. Only 3 minutes and 28 seconds into the extended game, quarterback Norm Van Brocklin led the Rams 70 yards down the field, and Younger plunged into the end zone for a 2-yard touchdown, sealing the Rams' victory. Although the preseason game was neither televised nor witnessed by many people, the experiment set the stage for the overtime rule, which the NFL finally adopted in 1974.

helped St. Louis rally to tie the game and force overtime. The score remained tied until the first snap in double-overtime, when Carolina quarterback Jake Delhomme hit receiver Steve Smith for a 69-yard touchdown to end the Rams' season.

Behind powerful rookie running back Steven Jackson, who had replaced Faulk as the team's top rusher, the 2004 Rams became the first 8–8 team ever to win a playoff game. The Rams overcame the Seattle Seahawks 27–20, with Bulger tossing two touchdown passes and Faulk rushing for a score. But the Atlanta Falcons crushed their Super Bowl hopes a week later, pummeling St. Louis 47–17.

The Rams then began to struggle, dropping to 6–10 in 2005. New coach Scott Linehan oversaw an 8–8 season in 2006. Then, in 2007, the team was plagued by injuries, limping to a 3–13 record. "You have to acknowledge it happened," Coach Linehan said of the disappointing year, "but the first priority is to look in a positive way ahead to what we can get done and give ourselves the best chance to have great success next year."

In the 2008 NFL Draft, the Rams took their first rebuilding step by selecting defensive end Chris Long with the second overall pick. Long, the son of Hall of Fame defensive end Howie Long, had been a star at the

X Playing in his 10th NFL season by 2008, sure-handed Torry Holt remained one of the game's most dangerous wide receivers.

MEET THE RAMS

MARSHALL FAULK

RUNNING BACK
RAMS SEASONS: 1999-2006
HEIGHT: 5-FOOT-10
WEIGHT: 211 POUNDS

Marshall Faulk burst onto the scene in St. Louis in 1999 after playing with the Indianapolis Colts for five years. At 5-foot-10, Faulk was smaller than most other running backs, but his size gave him a low center of gravity, and his powerful legs made it difficult for a single defender to bring him down. New York Giants linebacker Nick Greisen once described the difficulty of tackling Faulk. "One guy has him by the shirt, and all of a sudden he slips out of it," Greisen said. "You've got to have everybody, and don't expect he's down until the whistle blows." With the speed and sure hands of a wide receiver and the rare ability to change directions instantly, Faulk motored his way to 12,279 rushing yards and 100 rushing touchdowns during his career. He was named NFL Offensive Player of the Year three years in a row, from 1999 through 2001, and helped carry the Rams to the Super Bowl after the 1999 and 2001 seasons. Knee surgery kept him from playing the 2006 season, and he announced his retirement in 2007.

University of Virginia, notching 14 sacks during his senior

season. Although the Rams remained in the NFC West

cellar in 2008, fans hoped that Long and such other young

players as defensive tackle Adam Carriker would boost the

Rams back up the standings.

Success came early and often to the Rams, and they have

left their mark in every city they have called home, winning

an NFL championship in Cleveland, Los Angeles, and St. Louis.

Throughout the team's journey, it has also showcased such

crowd-pleasing players as Bob Waterfield, Crazylegs Hirsch,

and Marshall Faulk. Today, St. Louis fans are hoping that the

team with the curly-horned helmets will soon be king of the

NFL mountain again.

X Although St. Louis
ended the 2008 season
just 2–14, rising stars
such as defensive end
Chris Long planned to
restore the Rams as an
NFC power.

INDEX